"Inside you
there's an artist
you don't
know about."

RUMI

The life of a man is a circle from childhood to childhood, and so it is in everything where power moves. The life of a man is a circle from childhood to childhood, and so it is in everything where power moves. Even the seasons form a great circle in their changing, and always come back again to where they were. The sun comes forth and goes down again in a circle. The moon does the same, and both are round. Even the stars. The sky is round, and I have heard that the earth is round like a ball, and so are all the stars. Everything the Power of the World does is done in a circle. Birds make their nests in circles, for theirs is the same religion as ours. The wind, in its greatest power, whirls.

"

BLACK ELK

creativity

COLOR *yourself* CALM

Mandalas by
Paul Heussenstamm

BARRON'S

Introduction

Creativity

200 Horses

Blue Lotus

Blue Red Clouds

A Walk into the Sky

Breath of Fire

Catseye Terous

Cosmic Eggs

Dark Night of the Soul

Chagall Homage

Dionysia Flame

Four White Horses

Gold Shiva

High Dynamics

Instinctual Melody

Kali's Dance

Good Fortune

Love at the Door

Mango Moon

Mask of the Fox

Mexican Passion

Moonfire

Primal Voice

New Emerging Self Pansies

River Runs Through It

Resurrection of the
Wise Women

Origami

Rocket's Red Glare

Spheres of the Universe

The Penetration

Women at Balance

About the
quotes

About the
illustrator

INTRODUCTION

Welcome to the world of mandalas and the beginning of your journey to becoming more focused and centered by coloring your mind calm. This mindfulness-inspired coloring book includes 30 original color mandalas with their accompanying black-and-white templates to color in, which will expand your self-awareness and open the door into your own creativity.

Mandalas are an ancient form of meditative art. Simply put, the mandala is a design that draws your eye toward its center, which focuses your mind on the present moment and opens up your heart.

Within our fast-paced society, we are often in our minds rather than in our hearts—our minds then become closed to creativity, relaxation, or happiness. Once you begin to color in the mandalas, your center will begin to shift from your mind and into your heart. The core of the mandala then becomes the center of your heart. Importantly, once your heart is open your creativity naturally pours forth.

Coloring in mandalas relaxes the mind, body, and spirit; relieves stress; and is a chance to explore your own inner creativity. For the past 25 years, I have been exploring, painting, practicing, and teaching the art of mandala painting. The first thing you should know is that coloring mandalas requires no previous experience or innate artistic talent. As a teacher, the hardest task is to dispel the worries of students and banish any thoughts that they are not creative and are not naturally artistic.

The key to mandala coloring is to simply take the time to sit quietly, to focus your mind, and to begin coloring. This is precisely how I started my journey of coloring and painting mandalas way back in the late 1980s. At first, I did it for fun, but it then led to a profound change in my lifestyle. It makes no difference if you color in a single mandala or one thousand mandalas, it is merely the practice of centering yourself through creativity and relaxation, which ultimately leads to increased happiness.

Art is transformative. Mandala coloring transforms your attitude toward life and develops your consciousness. When you reach this meditative state through coloring, your body becomes more sensitive, your eyes see more deeply, and you will feel more intensely.

Congratulations on arriving at this point. You will now discover that as you begin to color in these mandalas your awareness will expand. As your awareness expands, and the more you color, you will begin to look and feel more deeply into the mandalas. Essentially, as you open up to see inside the mandala you are simultaneously opening up yourself.

A mandala is a very ancient guide that symbolically allows you to look into yourself. The process of coloring in a mandala can give you profound insights into your psyche and your mind. It appears simple, yet there are layers of growth, understanding, and even a transforming of consciousness that are revealed in a mandala painting, whether coloring one in or simply looking at one. The key to mandala meditation is to sit still and gaze at one. Once you have colored in several mandalas—or even several parts of one mandala—you will begin to feel and see patterns within yourself. This is deeply valuable because it allows you to recognize your own inner patterns and it helps you to communicate with your conscious self through the core patterns.

CREATIVITY

ACCEPTANCE

Participation in creative pursuits shifts your center from your mind to your heart, which increases your happiness. I have been teaching creative courses for the past 25 years and I always tell my students that when you take one of my workshops you must step outside of your conscious mind and open up your channels of creativity.

EXISTENCE

When you engage with this inner creativity, your otherwise narrow world is transformed into an infinite universe. When I am immersed in any creative process, I exist outside of time and space, but I equally feel incredibly connected to the universe as a whole.

CONNECTIVITY

On the deepest level, the artist is a conduit—the mandalas are paintings that are simply a passage for their creator. The beauty of creative pursuits is that once your heart is open and you are fully connected to the infinite universe, creativity naturally spills forth. Someone who has never considered himself/herself a creative can, in an instant, experience a shift in his/her existence.

TRANSFORMATION

Creativity can radically alter your perspective. The wonderful thing about coloring mandalas is that once you learn the practice, coloring is easily shareable with friends, with loved ones, and with children.

STILLNESS

When coloring mandalas, you can no longer think about blues, purples, or greens in the same way. Thoughts become colors. Colors become patterns. Patterns awaken the soul. Coloring becomes magic. From deep within, you will feel stillness and relaxation, because the colors shine through you. Your mind shifts from the logical and reasoning left brain to the intuitive and emotional right brain.

ATTAINMENT

As you begin to access your inner creativity, while also allowing yourself the time, patience, and focus to color yourself calm, your perspectives and outlook on life will change. Transformation is a form of happiness that wells up from your core being. This attainment of joy will most likely be beyond anything you have ever felt before.

TRANSMITTANCE

In becoming an artist, you are making something that you love, while also touching others on a very deep level. After you have colored in each of your chosen mandalas, take a photograph or scan your creation and share it on social media with the hashtag #coloryourselfcalm so that people all over the world can enjoy your creativity. This creates a form of shared happiness that no words can do justice.

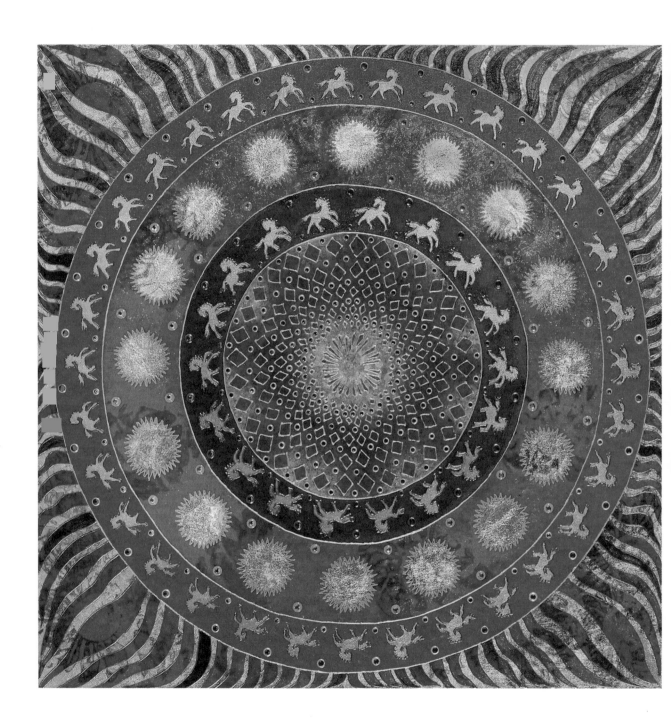

200 Horses

We are all creative. Everyone is!
It is important to release self-doubt,
judgment, and let creativity flow through you.

Blue Lotus

Blue Red Clouds

"*Painting is a blind man's profession. He paints not what he sees but what he feels, (and) what he tells himself about what he has seen.*"
PABLO PICASSO

A Walk into the Sky

Breath of Fire

"There are painters who transform the sun into a yellow spot, but there are others who with the help of their art and their intelligence, transform a yellow spot into the sun."

PABLO PICASSO

Catseye Teruos

Cosmic Eggs

"Colors became sticks of dynamite. They were primed to discharge light."
ANDRÉ DERAIN

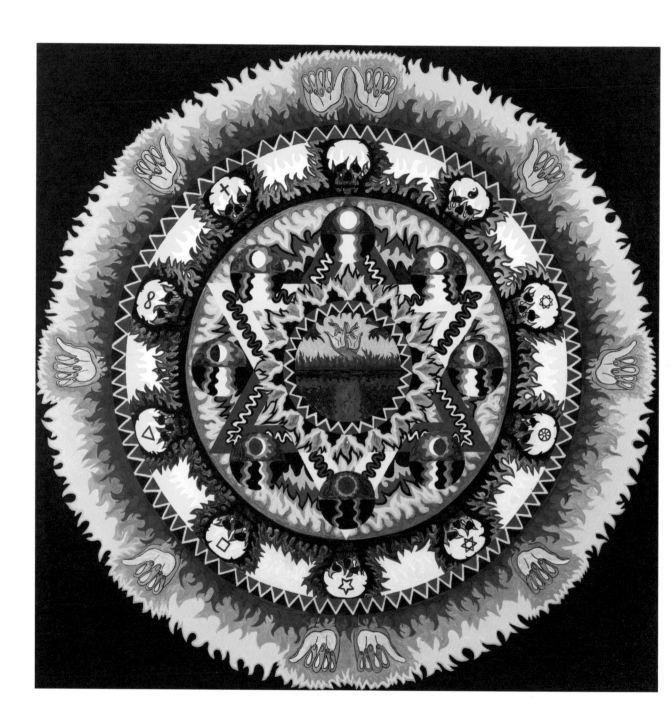

Dark Night of the Soul

Chagall Homage

"*If I create from the heart nearly everything works;*
if from the head, almost nothing."
MARC CHAGALL

Dionysia Flame

Four White Horses

The mandala is the key to manifestation.

Gold Shiva

High Dynamics

All the artists in the world, working together,
makes the creativity that exists in our universe.

Instinctual Melody

Kali's Dance

"My greatest desire is to learn how to change and re-create reality."
FRANCIS BACON

Good Fortune

Love at the Door

"*Today we are searching for things in nature that are hidden behind the veil of appearance… We look for and paint this inner, spiritual side of nature.*"
FRANZ MARC

Mango Moon

Mask of the Fox

*"The greater the artist, the greater the doubt. Perfect confidence
is granted to the less talented as a consolation prize."*
PAUL CÉZANNE

Mexican Passion

Moonfire

Art is the connection to all the creativity
woven into the infinite universe.

Primal Voice

New Emerging Self Pansies

"Creativity takes courage."
HENRI MATISSE

River Runs Through It

Resurrection of the Wise Women

The artist makes and creates atomic explosions of color.

Origami

Rocket's Red Glare

"The creation of works of art is the creation of the world."
WASSILY KANDINSKY

Spheres of the Universe

The Penetration

"Imagination is the mother of arts."
FRANCISCO DE GOYA

Women at Balance

QUOTES ARE TAKEN FROM:

RUMI was a thirteenth-century Persian poet, theologian, and Sufi mystic.

BLACK ELK was a famous holy man, traditional healer, and visionary of the North American tribe of Oglala Lakota (Sioux).

PABLO PICASSO was one of the greatest and most influential artists of the twentieth century, as well as the cocreator and leading exponent of Cubism.

ANDRÉ DERAIN was a French painter of the Fauvist school; a friend of Henri Matisse.

MARC CHAGALL was an early Modernist artist who worked in almost every medium to convey an expression of emotion as opposed to pictoral reality.

FRANCIS BACON was an English artist who is best known for his mid-twentieth-century paintings of tortured figures in an expressive, often grotesque style.

FRANZ MARC was a German print marker and artist in the early twentieth century, considered to be one of the key figures within the Expressionist movement.

PAUL CÉZANNE was a leading Post-Impressionist painter in early twentieth century France, who was celebrated for his progressive painting style that influenced abstract art.

HENRI MATISSE was an influential French artist of the early twentieth century, best known for his expressive use of color and form in the Fauvist style.

WASSILY KANDINSKY was a Russian-born painter who, as one of the founders of pure abstraction in painting, is credited as a leading exponent of avant-garde art in the early twentieth century.

FRANCISCO DE GOYA was a famed Spanish painter during the late 1700s and early 1800s, who painted portraits for the Spanish royal court as well as more subversive political works.

PAUL HEUSSENSTAMM

Paul Heussenstamm is a master painter of mandalas and other forms of spiritual paintings. He has painted and drawn over 1,000 mandalas and has taught worldwide for 25 years, as well as at his studio in California.

Since 1996, he has worked for the Chopra Center for Wellbeing, sharing his art at almost every major event that Deepak Chopra hosts. He is the sanctuary artist at the Agape International Spiritual Center in Culver City in California, which has 10,000 local members.

Publishing director Sarah Lavelle
Commissioning editor Lisa Pendreigh
Creative director Helen Lewis
Designer Emily Lapworth
Production director Vincent Smith
Production controller Stephen Lang

First edition for North America published in 2016
by Barron's Educational Series, Inc.

First published in 2015 by
Quadrille Publishing
www.quadrille.co.uk

Quadrille is an imprint of Hardie Grant.
www.hardiegrant.com.au

Design & layout © 2015
Quadrille Publishing

Text © Paul Heussenstamm
Mandalas designs © Paul Heussenstamm

All inquiries should be addressed to:
Barron's Educational Series, Inc.
250 Wireless Boulevard
Hauppauge, NY 11788
www.barronseduc.com

ISBN: 978-1-4380-0837-0

Printed in China

9 8 7 6 5 4 3 2 1

For best results, colored pencils are recommended.